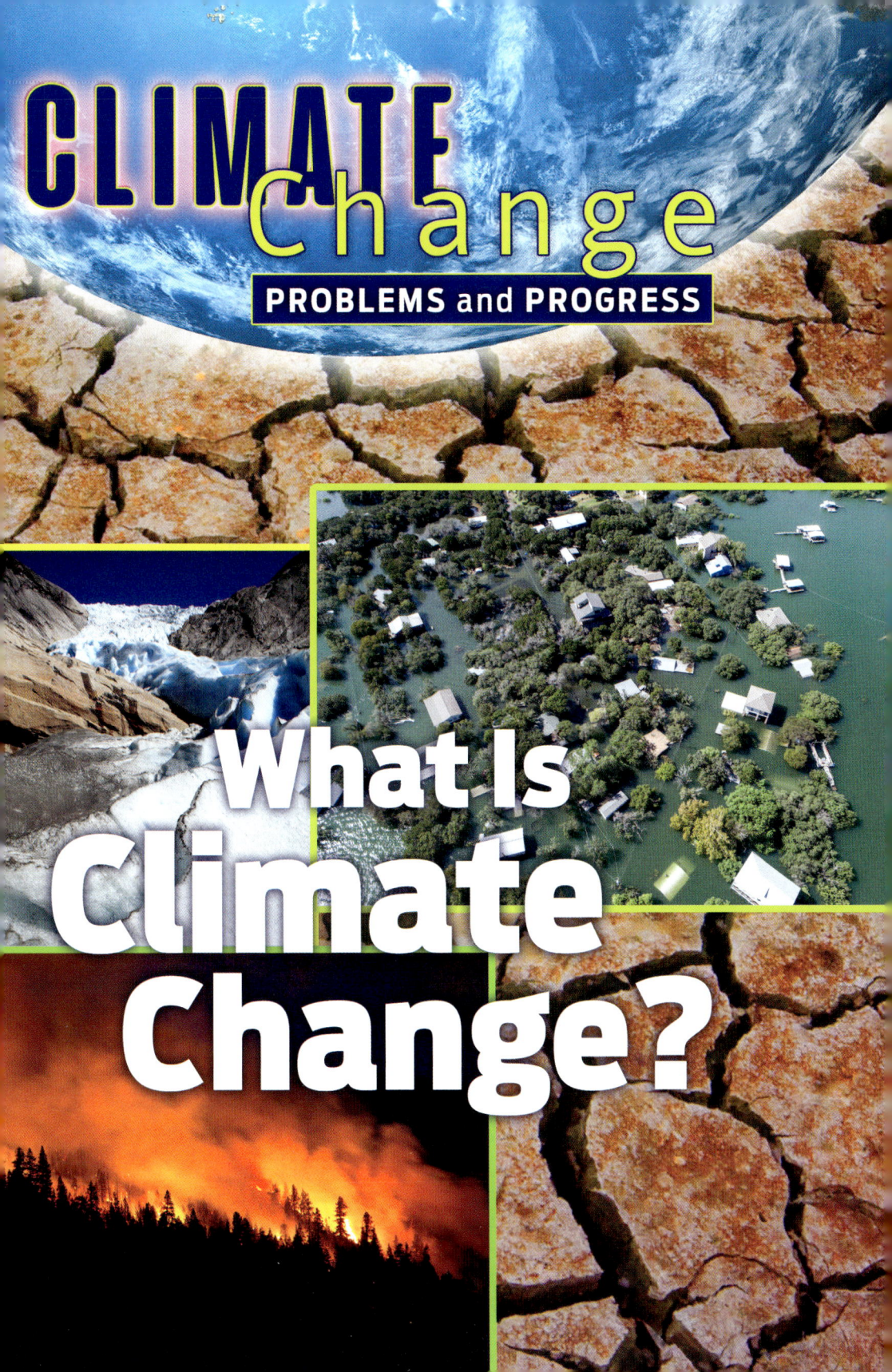

The Danger of Greenhouse Gases

Extreme Weather

The Future of Biodiversity

The Organic Lifestyle

Preserving Energy

Recycling Works!

Renewable Energy in Action

Saving Water

The Vital Role of Deserts and Forests

What Is Climate Change?

WITHDRAWN

What Is Climate Change?

James Shoals

Mason Crest

Mason Crest
450 Parkway Drive, Suite D
Broomall, PA 19008
www.masoncrest.com

© 2020 by Mason Crest, an imprint of National Highlights, Inc.

All rights reserved. No part of this publication may be reproduced or transmitted in any form or by any means, electronic or mechanical, including photocopying, recording, taping, or any information storage and retrieval system, without permission from the publisher.

Printed and bound in the United States of America.

Series ISBN: 978-1-4222-4353-4
Hardback ISBN: 978-1-4222-4363-3
EBook ISBN: 978-1-4222-7458-3

First printing
1 3 5 7 9 8 6 4 2

Cover photographs by Dreamstime.com: Dreamstime: Vadim Kozlovsky (bkgd.); Kippy Spiker (bottom); Svetlana Privezentseva (left); Bryan Roschetzky (right).

Library of Congress Cataloging-in-Publication Data
Names: Shoals, James, author. Title: What is climate change? / by James Shoals.
Description: Broomall, PA : Mason Crest, [2019] | Series: Climate challenges: problems and progress | Includes bibliographical references and index.
Identifiers: LCCN 2019013902| ISBN 9781422243633 (hardback) | ISBN 9781422243534 (series) | ISBN 9781422274583 (ebook)
Subjects: LCSH: Climatic changes--Juvenile literature. | Nature--Effect of human beings on--Juvenile literature. | Environmental responsibility--Juvenile literature. | Natural disasters--Juvenile literature.
Classification: LCC QC903.15 .S56 2019 | DDC 363.7--dc23 LC record available at https://lccn.loc.gov/2019013902

QR Codes disclaimer:
You may gain access to certain third party content ("Third-Party Sites") by scanning and using the QR Codes that appear in this publication (the "QR Codes"). We do not operate or control in any respect any information, products, or services on such Third-Party Sites linked to by us via the QR Codes included in this publication, and we assume no responsibility for any materials you may access using the QR Codes. Your use of the QR Codes may be subject to terms, limitations, or restrictions set forth in the applicable terms of use or otherwise established by the owners of the Third-Party Sites. Our linking to such Third-Party Sites via the QR Codes does not imply an endorsement or sponsorship of such Third-Party Sites, or the information, products, or services offered on or through the Third-Party Sites, nor does it imply an endorsement or sponsorship of this publication by the owners of such Third-Party Sites.

CONTENTS

Words to Understand 6
Introduction 8
Greenhouse Effect 10
The Ozone Hole 12
Natural Causes 14
El Niño and La Niña 16
Human Influences 18
Deaths and Diseases 20
Natural Disasters 22
Impact on Agriculture 24
Impact on Wildlife 26
Impact on Coral Reefs 28
Impact on Forests 30

Impact on Bodies of Water 32
Impact on Drinking Water 34
Polar Regions 36
International Treaties 38
Climate in the Future 40
Adaptation 42

Text-Dependent Questions 44
Research Projects 45
Find Out More 46
Series Glossary of Key Terms 47
Index 48

KEY ICONS TO LOOK FOR

 Words to Understand: These words with their easy-to-understand definitions will increase the reader's understanding of the text, while building vocabulary skills.

 Sidebars: This boxed material within the main text allows readers to build knowledge, gain insights, explore possibilities, and broaden their perspectives by weaving together additional information to provide realistic and holistic perspectives.

 Educational Videos: Readers can view videos by scanning our QR codes, providing them with additional educational content to supplement the text. Examples include news coverage, moments in history, speeches, iconic moments, and much more!

 Text-Dependent Questions: These questions send the reader back to the text for more careful attention to the evidence presented here.

 Research Projects: Readers are pointed toward areas of further inquiry connected to each chapter. Suggestions are provided for projects that encourage deeper research and analysis.

 Series Glossary of Key Terms: This back-of-the-book glossary contains terminology used throughout this series. Words found here increase the reader's ability to read and comprehend higher-level books and articles in this field.

WORDS TO UNDERSTAND

abrupt sudden

barren having little or no vegetation; desolate and lifeless

biodiversity the diversity of plant and animal life in a habitat (or in the world as a whole)

bulkhead a partition that divides a ship or aircraft into compartments

dike a barrier constructed to contain the flow of water or to keep out the sea

diversity the variety of things

drastic extreme effect

ecosystem refers to a community of organisms, their interaction with each other, and their physical environment

famine a severe shortage of food (as through crop failure) resulting in violent hunger, starvation, and death

hibernation a state of deep sleep in which an animal's heart rate and breathing slow down

kiloyear the unit of time equal to 1,000 years

potable suitable for drinking

precipitation the water that falls on the ground in the form of rain, snow, hail, sleet, or mist

protocol the original copy of any official document, for example, an agreement

rainforest a forest with heavy annual rainfall

runoff the occurrence of surplus liquid (as water)

symbiotic the interaction between organisms (especially of different species) that live together and happen to benefit from each other

troposphere the lowest atmospheric layer; from 6 to 9 km high

INTRODUCTION

Climate refers to the average weather pattern of a particular area. Weather is the state of the atmosphere of a particular region. The factors that contribute to the weather of a given place are rainfall, temperature, air pressure, and humidity. Weather changes every day. Climate change, however, is a much more complex phenomenon, with great consequences on ecology.

The rise in global temperatures over the decades has proved that climate is indeed changing. Much of this change is attributed to various human activities. Adapting to climate change is not always easy, but there is no alternative than to adjust. To prevent further damage, people need to adopt a more responsible attitude toward nature and restrict the activities that harm it in the longer run.

Climate in the Past

About 2.7 billion years ago, the earth experienced its first glacial period known as the first ice age. During this period, everything was covered in thick ice sheets. Then the planet warmed up until another ice age began about 850 million years ago. The last ice age ended about 11,000 years ago, beginning the present period known as the Holocene Epoch.

The Younger Dryas

About 14,500 years ago, the earth's temperature began to change from a glacial state to a warmer state (interglacial). However, the climate again changed to glacial conditions for a brief period. This period is called the Younger Dryas. It lasted for about 1,200 to 1,300 years and occurred around 12,800 to 11,500 years ago.

8.2 Kiloyear Event

The earth's temperature started rising at the beginning of the Holocene Period. However, around 8,200 years ago, the climate changed abruptly and the planet cooled down. This lasted for about two to four centuries. Thereafter, the temperatures returned to the previous state. Scientists called this **abrupt** cooling of earth the 8.2 K event.

The Little Ice Age

Between the sixteenth and the mid-nineteenth centuries, the global temperature was about 3°F (1.6°C) cooler than it is in the present times. During this period, there was widespread **famine**, and agriculture suffered. There were violent storms that caused loss of life. Despite the cold climate, it cannot be called an ice age since it did not last long enough for the ice sheets to expand.

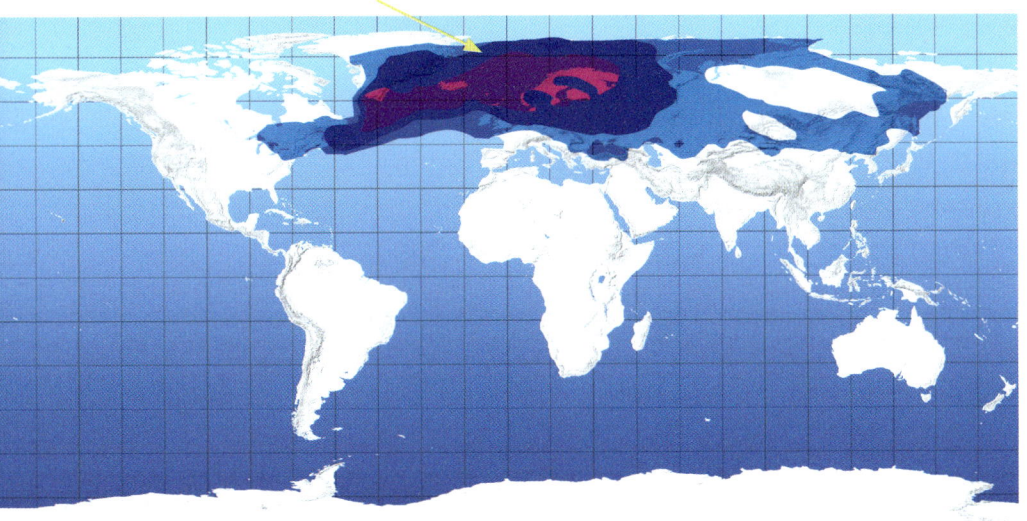

THE YOUNGER DRYAS COOLING

Climate Facts

- Since 1880, the global temperature has risen by 1.4°F (0.7°C).

- The Younger Dryas got its name from a flower called *Dryas octopetala*, which grows in cold climate.

What Is Climate Change? 9

Greenhouse Effect

When sunrays reach the earth, they are reflected back toward the sun. However, the greenhouse gases (GHGs) present in the atmosphere trap some of the outgoing radiation. This causes the earth to warm up. The GHGs prevent heat from escaping into space and keeps the earth warm enough to sustain life. This is called the greenhouse effect.

Greenhouse Gases

Water vapor, nitrous oxide (N_2O), carbon dioxide (CO_2), ozone (O_3) and methane (CH_4) are some of the naturally occurring GHGs. Chlorofluorocarbon (CFC) is a man-made GHG. Human activities are also responsible for the emissions of N_2O and CH_4. Since the Industrial Revolution, there has been a significant rise in the levels of man-made GHGs in the atmosphere. The vapor trailing from airplanes, soot rising from fires as well as the tropospheric ozone created by local pollution is intensifying the greenhouse effect.

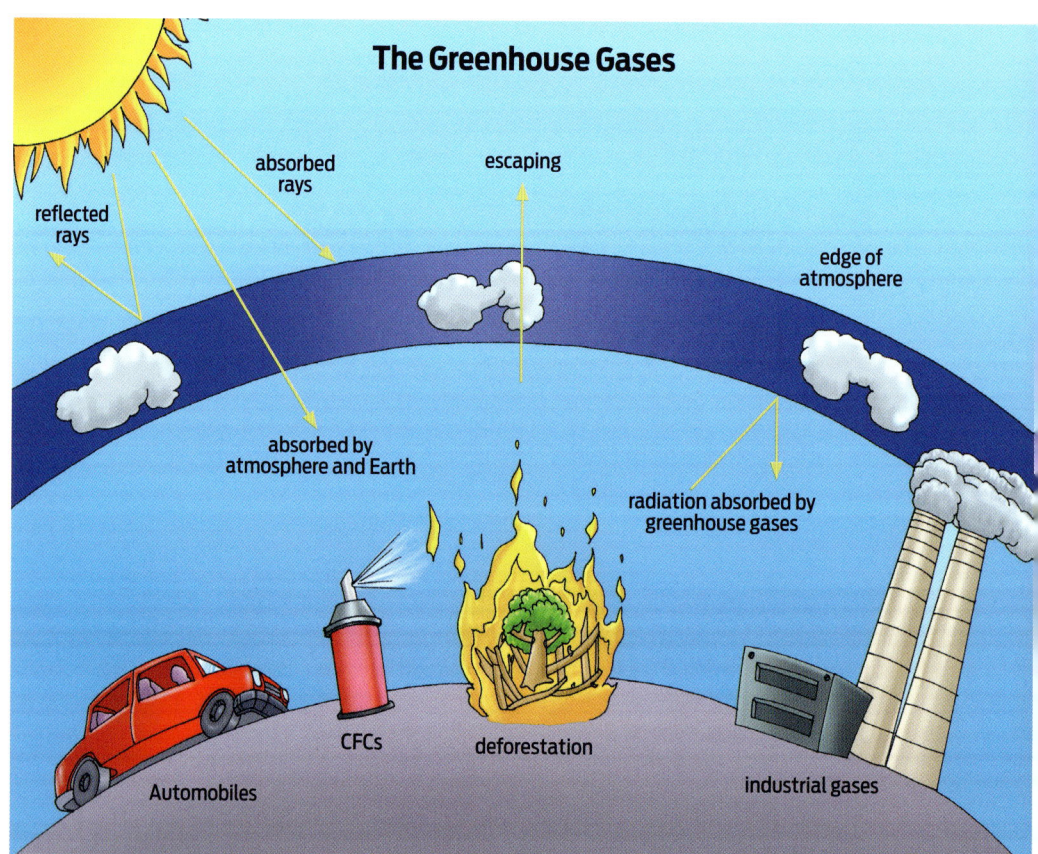

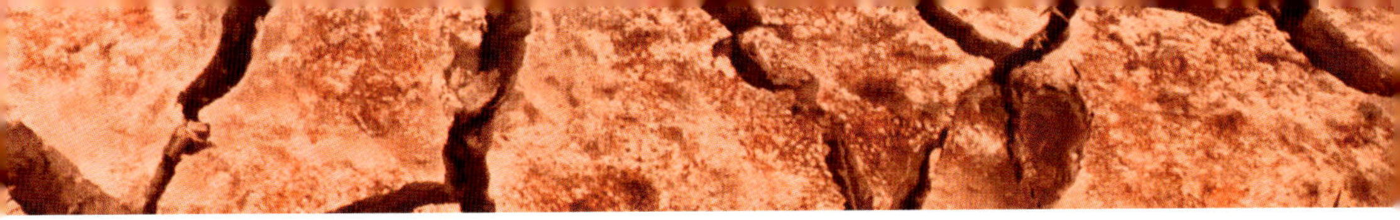

Carbon Cycle

CO_2 is very important for life on earth. Humans and animals inhale O_2 (oxygen) and exhale CO_2 (carbon dioxide) during respiration, while plants absorb that CO_2 and release O_2 during photosynthesis. This is how the carbon cycle maintains the CO_2 balance on earth. CO_2 is released into the air by other means as well, which is absorbed by the oceans. Each day, the carbon content in the air is increasing due to human activities, such as the burning of fossil fuels and wood, by deforestation, by pollution, and so on. This is causing an increase in global temperatures and causing global climate change.

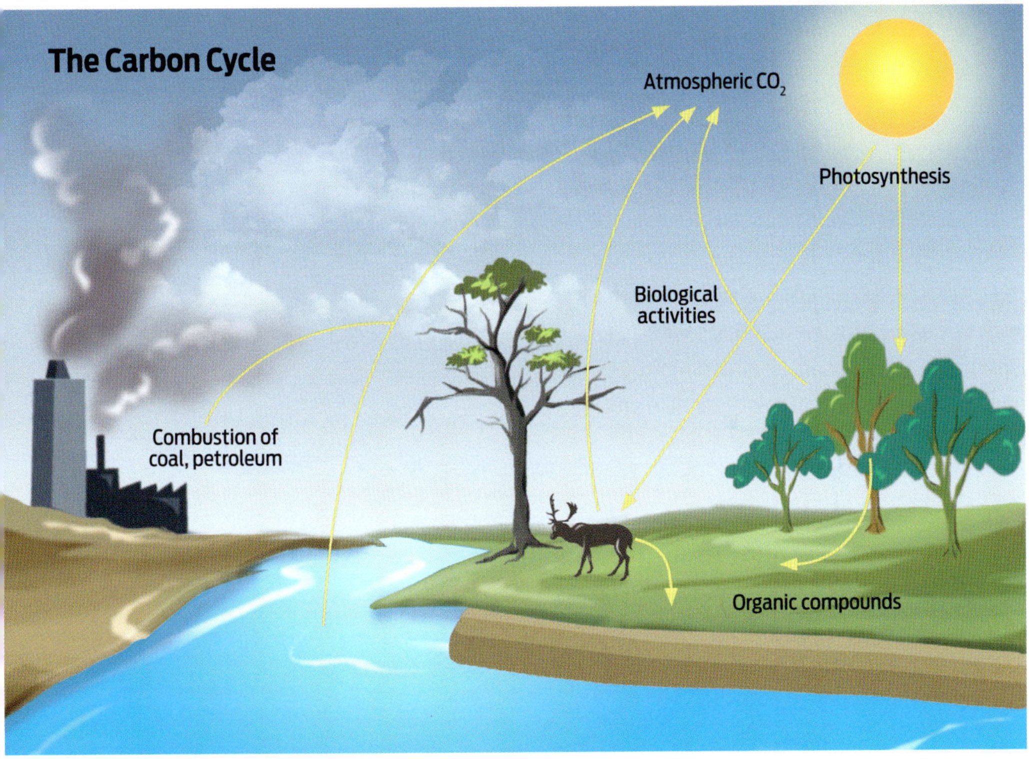

The Carbon Cycle

Climate Facts

- In 1824, French mathematician, Joseph Fourier, discovered the greenhouse effect.

- The Mauna Loa Observatory (MLO) in Hawaii monitors and collects data about atmospheric carbon dioxide

What Is Climate Change?   11

The Ozone Hole

Ozone (O_3) is a naturally occurring gas that, along with other gases, forms the earth's atmosphere. It absorbs almost 90 percent of the harmful ultraviolet B (UVB) radiation from the sun, thus providing living beings with a shield against UVB rays. Excessive exposure to UVB rays causes diseases such as skin cancer in humans, and also causes glacial melting.

The Ozone Hole

In the 1970s, scientists noticed the depletion of the ozone layer over the South Pole. Man-made GHGs such as the CFCs found in refrigerators, halons found in fire extinguishers, and hydrochlorofluorocarbons (HCFCs) are responsible for the depletion of ozone. When these gases reach the stratosphere, UV rays break them up and release chlorine atoms. A single chlorine atom is capable of destroying 100,000 ozone molecules, causing great damage to the ozone layer.

Ozone hole above Antarctica

Arctic Ozone Hole

In 2011, scientists confirmed the formation of an ozone hole over the Arctic as well. Long-lasting, extremely cold conditions and the surge of ozone-depleting substances are responsible for the loss of ozone. Cooling of the ozone layer in the Arctic increases the effect of CFCs, which destroy the ozone.

The Montreal Protocol

The Montreal Protocol on Substances that Deplete the Ozone Layer is an international treaty that was signed by 46 members of the United Nations. Various countries agreed to reduce, over time, the substances that can deplete the ozone layer and replace these substances with ozone-friendly substances. The treaty was opened for signatures on September 16, 1987. It went into effect January 1, 1989.

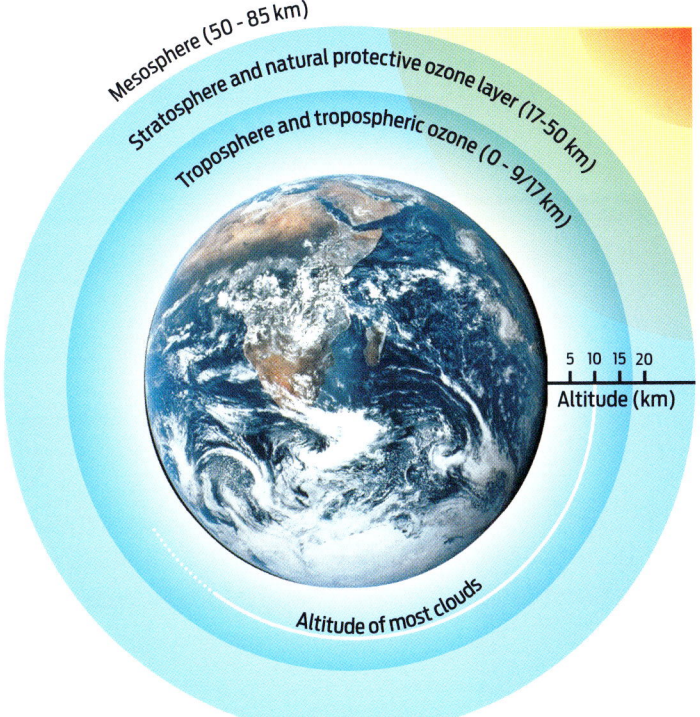

Troposphere: 0-5.5/10 miles
Stratosphere: 10-31 miles
Mesophere: 31-52 miles

Tibet Ozone Hole

In 2006, scientific research confirmed the presence of a 962,000 square miles (2.5 million sq km) hole in the low-level ozone layer over western China's Qinghai-Tibet Plateau. In 2011, an ozone hole developed over the mountainous regions of Tibet, Xinxiang, Qinghai, and the Hindu Kush.

Climate Facts

- By 2050, the ozone layer may heal completely as the usage of ozone-depleting substances has reduced drastically.

- About 7-10 percent of the ozone layer above the United States has depleted.

What Is Climate Change?

Natural Causes

Climate change occurs due to both manmade and natural causes. Though natural causes may not cause drastic changes in the climate, they make a permanent impact. Millions of years ago, when the landmasses drifted to form the present-day continents, they also changed the course of the ocean currents. This, in turn, changed the climate of the world.

Earth's Orbit

Every few thousands of years, changes in the earth's tilt and its orbit affect its climate. Seasons on earth are caused due to the tilt of the earth's axis. A change in the degree of the tilt would lead to a **drastic** change in the seasons. It may lead to warmer summers and colder winters, or have the opposite effect. The changes in the earth's orbit (every 100,000 years) and the earth's axial tilt (every 41,000 years) affect the amount of sunlight received by the earth's surface. This causes drastic climate change, such as the occurrence of ice ages. These observations were made by Milutin Milanković, a Serbian mathematician.

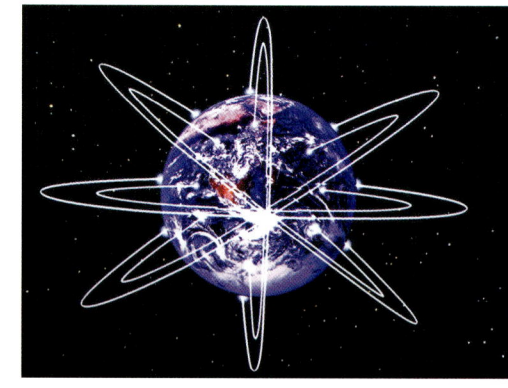

Solar Variation

Every 11 years, the sun goes through a cycle of activity, from stormy to quiet and then vice versa. This solar activity is caused by concentrated magnetic fields on the sun. When the solar activity is high, that is, during solar maximum, the solar radiation level is much higher. In contrast, solar irradiance has lower levels during solar maximum. These fluctuations bring a change of about 0.18°F (0.1°C) on the earth, slightly hotter during solar maximum and slightly cooler during solar minimum.

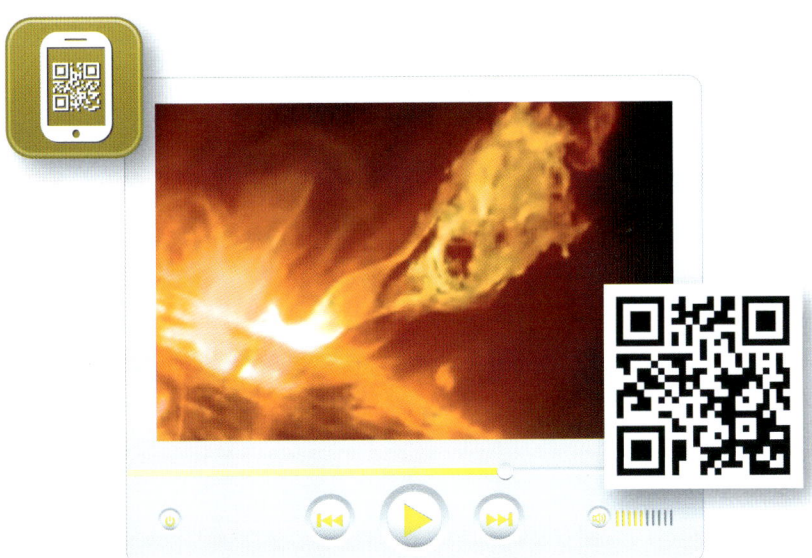

Solar flares explained

Climate Facts

- The volcanic eruption of Mount Pinatubo in 1991 released about 20 million tons of sulfur that led to the cooling of the lower **troposphere** for the following two years.

- The earth changes its tilt once every 41,000 years.

What Is Climate Change?   15

El Niño and La Niña

El Niño-Southern Oscillation (ENSO) is a natural climate pattern that occurs every five to eight years near the Pacific Ocean. It causes the sea surface temperature near the equator to rise higher than usual. During the La Niña event, the sea surface temperature of the same area gets colder than usual. Both these events greatly affect the climate patterns of other parts of the world as well.

Effect of El Niño

The El Niño event particularly changes the climate of the northern hemisphere. It causes heavy rainfall in South America, floods from Ecuador to the Gulf of Mexico, and hurricanes in Hawaii and Tahiti. At the same time, it causes severe droughts in some areas such as Central America and Australia. It even causes winters to be warmer than usual in the eastern United States.

Effect of La Niña

The La Niña event reverses the effects of El Niño. It causes droughts in South America and extensive floods and rainfalls in eastern Australia. The winters are colder and drier than usual during this period. Marine animals enjoy their meals during La Niña as the currents bring nutrients that have settled deep under water to the surface.

Global Warming and Weather Events

Due to global warming, ocean currents and weather systems are not able to release the extra heat collected in the tropical seas. Climate scientists have suggested that warmer ocean temperatures have increased the intensity and frequency of El Niño and La Niña events in recent decades. Higher temperatures can potentially increase evaporation from land and add moisture to the air, which intensifies the storms and floods triggered by El Niño.

Climate Facts

- *El Niño* means "the boy" and *La Niña* means "the girl" in Spanish.

- The 1997–98 ENSO was the strongest in the last 50 years.

What Is Climate Change? 17

Human Influences

Human activities have had an enormous influence on global warming. Every day, humans cause the emission of strong GHGs like carbon dioxide and methane, which enhances the greenhouse (GH) effect. Different GHGs have different heat-trapping capacities. Therefore, human activities are partially responsible for the changes in world climate.

Overpopulation

Due to the increasing population, fossil fuels are being overused to meet human needs. The energy produced by burning them is used to generate electricity, run automobiles, and power factories. These activities release enormous amounts of CO_2 into the environment. The CO_2 thus generated accounts for almost three-quarters of the total CO_2 emissions caused by human activities.

Deforestation

The growth of industrial activities has resulted in large-scale deforestation. An increasing number of trees are felled for use by the wood, paper, and other industries, without replanting new ones. Massive deforestation has increased the amount of CO_2 in the atmosphere. With fewer trees to absorb the excess CO_2, the GHG effect is increasing. As a result, the global warming phenomenon continues to worsen.

18 CLIMATE CHANGE: Problems and Progress

Industrial Emissions

Since the beginning of the Industrial Revolution in the 1800s, there has been an enormous growth of GHGs in the atmosphere. The industrial and transportation sectors are chiefly responsible for increasing CO_2 in the atmosphere. In the last 150 years, the CO_2 content in the air has increased to 379 parts per million (ppm) from 280 ppm due to industrial emissions. Vehicles in the US alone add about 1.7 billion tons of CO_2 to the atmosphere every year.

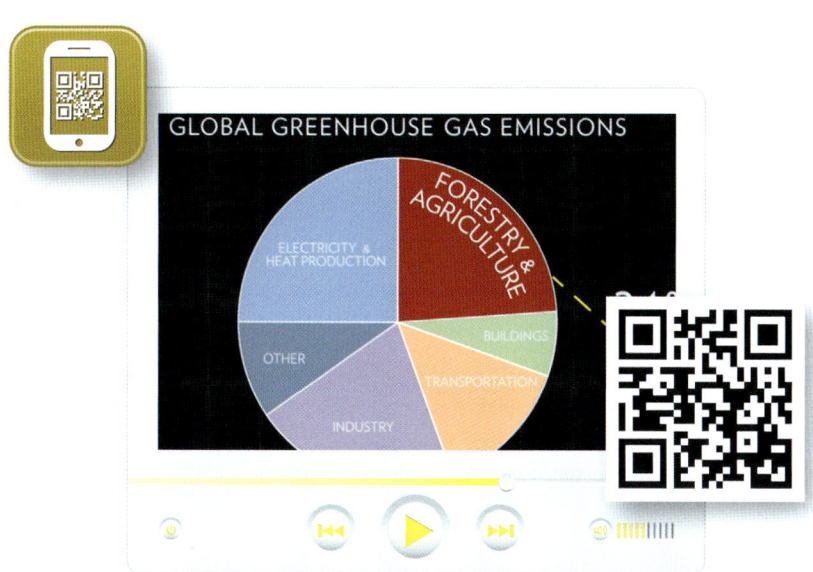

Impact of deforestation on climate change

Climate Facts

- Since 1959, global CO_2 concentration in the air has increased from 316 parts per million to 392 ppm in 2011.

- **Rainforests** absorb about 20 percent of the atmospheric carbon.

What Is Climate Change?   19

Deaths and Diseases

Climate change poses a serious threat to human health. As the global temperature increases, humans struggle to cope with its effects. Though they are adapting to the atmospheric changes, the rapidity of climate change is posing new health challenges. Higher temperatures are increasing heat-related illnesses and diseases.

Respiratory Problems

Climate change increases smog (ground-level ozone) that contains harmful particles, causing severe damage to the respiratory system upon inhalation. It reduces lung capacity and worsens asthma. High temperatures also cause the pollen season to start early. The allergenic pollen produced by weedy plant species increases the discomfort of people suffering from respiratory disorders.

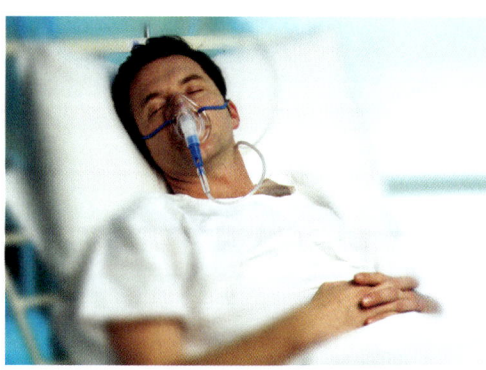

Illnesses and Deaths

Due to rising temperatures, people are suffering from numerous heat-related illnesses, such as heatstroke, heat cramps, high body temperatures, and heat exhaustion. Extreme heat can even cause death. Infants, the elderly, and the sick are at a higher risk. Between 1998 and 2011, about 500 children died due to heatstroke in the United States during the summer months.

CLIMATE CHANGE: Problems and Progress

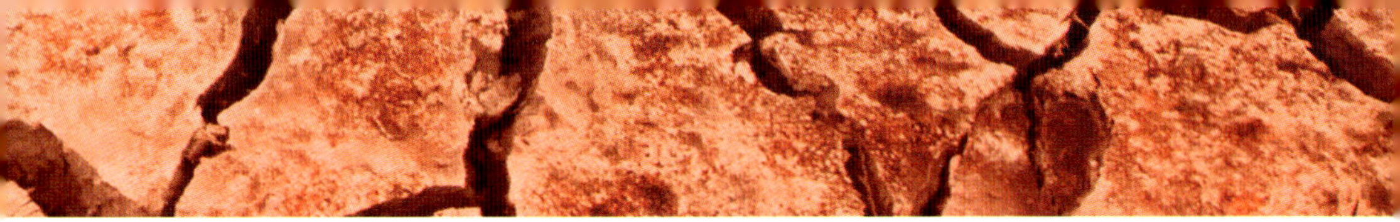

Climate-sensitive Diseases

Climate change is increasing the spread of vector-borne diseases, especially those that occur in warmer regions and are transmitted by mosquitoes and other insects. Deadly diseases like malaria, dengue fever, and yellow fever are increasing daily. The increase in rainfall as well as in temperature also lengthen the disease-transmission period.

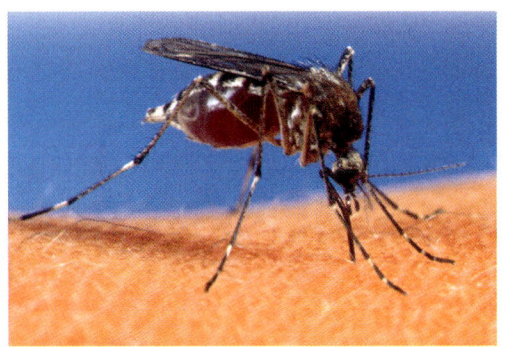

Report on climate impact on health

Climate Facts

- About 19,000 people died in the 2010 summer heat wave in the Northern Hemisphere.

- Worldwide, about 1 million people die of malaria and 30,000 people of yellow fever every year.

What Is Climate Change?   21

Natural Disasters

The frequency of natural disasters such as tsunamis, hurricanes, earthquakes, floods, and heat waves has increased tremendously since the last century due to climate change. The Rio de Janeiro floods (2011), the Japan earthquake and tsunami (2012), the Nepal earthquake (2015), and the fierce California wildfires (2017-18), were all results of—or were made more deadly by—climate change.

Heat Waves

James Hanson, a top United States scientist, recently suggested that the deadly European heat wave of 2003 and the Russian heat wave of 2010 can both be linked to climate change and global warming. Studies on climate change repeatedly suggest that heat waves have increased in recent years due to searing heat. A recent study has indicated that changes in rainfall patterns lead to soil dryness, which is an indicator of an impending heat wave.

Hurricanes

Hurricanes are tropical storms that occur when the ocean water warms up, evaporates, and mixes with strong winds. Hurricanes get their energy from the warming oceans. As oceans warm due to climate change, the occurrence of severe hurricanes rises.

Floods and Droughts

As temperatures increase, so does the amount of water vapor in the atmosphere. This causes higher levels of **precipitation**. In some areas, heavy rainfalls raise water levels in rivers and lakes, causing extreme flooding. Some areas, however, experience less rainfall, which leads to severe droughts. Lands become dry and **barren** and the water resources such as rivers, lakes, and ponds dry up.

Climate Facts

- The 2003 European heat wave killed more than 30,000 people all over the continent.

- In 1933-35, the Great Plains of North America suffered a major drought.

What Is Climate Change?   23

Impact on Agriculture

Agriculture largely depends on climatic conditions. Warmer temperatures interfere with the production of certain crops and increase the growth of weeds and pests. The changes in precipitation patterns also cause crop failures. While humans are developing new technologies to increase crop productivity, climate change is acting as a major hindrance.

Changing Crop Seasons

The rising temperature is greatly affecting crop growth in those regions where high temperatures persist, for example, in California, where the production of wine grapes is decreasing. However, crop production in cold climatic regions, such as the Great Lakes region and Canada, is increasing due to an extended growth season.

CO$_2$ Fertilization

Although CO$_2$ is a GHG, it acts as a positive factor for the agricultural sector. Higher concentrations of atmospheric CO$_2$ due to human activities play the role of a fertilizer and enhance the production of crops like soybeans, rice, and wheat. This process is called CO$_2$ fertilization. However, crops also need adequate water supply and other nutrients like nitrates. Climate change affects their concentration, thus affecting agriculture.

Changing Rainfall Patterns

Precipitation patterns change drastically due to climate change. Areas near bodies of water experience more rainfall, as the hot climate increases evaporation causing the formation of clouds. In other remote areas, extreme temperatures increase the rate of soil evaporation and cause droughts. In both events, the soil quality is affected and crop production suffers.

Climate Facts

- Annually, about 3.5 million people die worldwide due to malnutrition caused by droughts.

- It is projected that by 2030, South Africa will face about 31 percent reduction in its main crop, corn, due to climate change.

What Is Climate Change? 25

Impact on Wildlife

Global warming and the changing climate is affecting wildlife by forcing animals to change their habitats and migration patterns. In fact, many species are facing the threat of extinction. Climate change disrupts the life cycle, reproduction rate and timing, as well as the feeding behaviors of animals.

Mammals

Mammals around the world are experiencing changes in their breeding and **hibernation** patterns. Their size is changing due to rising temperatures, less food availability, and lifestyle changes. Polar bears that move around on floating ice to hunt, and seals that give birth, nurse, and rest their babies on snow, are facing serious danger due to the melting summer sea ice.

Birds

Migratory birds have started making early stops in cold regions due to warmer climate and have also started early breeding and nesting. Their early arrival, however, does not guarantee the availability of insects on which they depend for food. Similar situations are affecting other birds as well.

Fish and Amphibians

Rising temperatures are affecting the quality of bodies of water. This interferes with the productivity of fish and amphibians, as well as their **diversity**. For example, in high winter temperatures, the eggs of yellow perch, a cold-water species, do not survive. Many salamander and frog species lay their eggs in pools formed after snowmelt. However, those pools dry out in hot weather, which affects the animals' population growth.

Climate Facts

- Due to climate change, the harlequin frog and the golden toad found in Costa Rica are now extinct.

- In the past 30 years, the breeding pairs of Adélie penguins in Antarctica have reduced from 30,000 to 11,000.

What Is Climate Change?

Impact on Coral Reefs

Coral reefs are structures under the oceans made up of calcium carbonate deposited by shellfish, coralline algae, and corals. These colorful reefs are a natural habitat for almost 25 percent of marine life in the world. They protect coastal regions from storm waves and are a major tourist attraction worldwide.

Coral Bleaching

Coral reefs are under threat due to climate change. Corals live in a **symbiotic** relationship with zooxanthellae algae, which also give color to corals. The algae make food through the process of photosynthesis, which they share with corals. Corals, on the other hand, provide shelter and light to the algae. Warmer temperatures are forcing many corals to expel their zooxanthellae algae, causing them to lose their color along with the algae, exposing the white calcium carbonate colonies. This is called coral bleaching.

CLIMATE CHANGE: Problems and Progress

Great Barrier Reef Bleaching

The 1997-98 El Niño weather events caused the temperature in the Great Barrier Reef in Australia to rise by about 2°C. Coral bleaching on the reef happened due to extreme hot weather in Australia that lasted two weeks. The effects were quite severe. This caused massive coral bleaching, affecting 87 percent of inshore reefs.

The bad news continues for the largest coral reef in the world. By 2018, *National Geographic* reported that half of the reef had died due to warming ocean temperatures. It is estimated that if the ocean temperatures continue to rise, the Great Barrier Reef may lose about 95 percent of its corals by 2050.

Climate Facts

- Coral bleaching was first observed in the 1990s in the South Pacific.

- More than 92 percent of the Florida Keys' coral reefs have undergone bleaching since 1975.

What Is Climate Change?

Impact on Forests

After the end of the last ice age, trees adapted to a temperature rise of about 3.6 to 5.4°F (2 to 3°C). Before the end of this century, global temperatures are expected to rise by 2.7° to 3.6°F (1.5 to 2.5°C). Adapting to such rapid climate change would affect forests worldwide. Forests and forest soils store more than one trillion tons of carbon—twice the amount present in the atmosphere.

Changes in Growth

High temperature is decreasing the growth and productivity of boreal forests found in high-altitude regions. Tropical forests, however, have already adapted to high temperatures. Forests in temperate regions are giving way to new species of trees that are best suited to new climates. In areas where climate change is causing a decrease in precipitation, forests are dying out and giving way to shrubs and grasslands.

Economic Effect

It is predicted that forest productivity in the United States may increase due to climate change, thus increasing timber production. This might bring down the price of timber in future. Outdoor camps that offer sports such as fishing, hiking, hunting, camping, and others, would profit more due to the increased growth of forests.

Forest Fires

Forests tend to be prone to outbreaks of fire. Rising temperatures are making soils and trees drier, are causing more lightning, and thus increasing the risk of fire. In addition, climate change is increasing the population of insects and pests that destroy forest vegetation. Millions of trees around the world are destroyed by pests. Forest fires, insects, and pests are affecting the growth of forests and putting pressure on the **ecosystem**.

Climate Facts

- In 1987, the Amazon rainforest caught fire, resulting in the emission of about 500 million tons of CO_2 into the environment.

- The northern boreal forests cover about 5.8 million acres (1.5 billion hectares).

What Is Climate Change?

Impact on Bodies of Water

One of the grave effects of global warming is the shrinking of freshwater bodies due to the high rate of evaporation. It is also responsible for the rapid melting of polar ice, the rise in the level of oceans and seas and is affecting the quality of marine waters. The water cycle, an important natural phenomenon, is also experiencing disturbances.

Ocean Acidification

Oceans absorb about one-third of the atmospheric CO_2 and deposit it into the deep, where it forms carbonic acid. This increases the oceans' acidity. The excess acidification of oceans will have a major impact on the marine ecosystem. Certain marine species will find it difficult to survive as this acidification worsens.

Glaciers and Ice Sheets

Glaciers are extremely slow-moving rivers of ice. They cover about 10 percent of the global land area and are the largest reservoirs of fresh water. Due to rising temperatures, they are melting rapidly and causing the loss of ice mass. For example, glacial ice on Mount Kilimanjaro in Africa has reduced by 80 percent in the last century.

32 CLIMATE CHANGE: Problems and Progress

Rise in Sea Levels

The level of seas is increasing for two reasons. The first is the expansion of seawater due to the warming of the oceans. Secondly, the melting of glaciers and sea ice from Antarctica and Greenland is adding to the rise. Rising sea levels are a major threat to about two-thirds of the global cities located on coastal regions.

Climate Facts
- From 1993 to 2003, the average rate of global sea level rise was 0.12 inches (3.1 mm) per year.
- During the second half of the 20th century, sea levels rose by about 1 inch (2.5 cm) due to thermal expansion.

What Is Climate Change? 33

Impact on Drinking Water

Although 75 percent of the earth is covered with water, there is a shortage of drinking water. Less than 1 percent of the earth's water is drinkable. Most of it is locked in the ice sheets of Antarctica and Greenland, leaving a small amount for drinking and agricultural purposes. Rapid changes in climate are affecting the availability of drinking water.

More Demand, Less Supply

Currently about one-fifth of the global population is experiencing water shortage. The rate of water usage is twice the rate of population growth. In almost 75 percent of Chinese cities, the demand for water is higher than its supply, and Africa suffers from year-round water shortages. Freshwater sources are reducing due to climate change. Glaciers in the Himalayas are also shrinking.

Saltwater Intrusion

As the sea levels are likely to rise further due to global warming, the saline water from seas would mix with the coastal freshwater aquifers. Additionally, the groundwater in aquifers is depleting faster than they can recharge. This is likely to cause shortages of drinking water in the future.

Low Quality of Water

Increasing temperatures are causing more precipitation, but **potable** water is not increasing. Freshwater bodies are cleansed naturally by some organisms, but the oxygen content decreases in warm water, affecting the population of such organisms. Excessive rainfall cause **runoffs** of harmful contaminants from land into rivers, making the water unfit for drinking. Municipal sewer systems may overflow during extreme rainfall, forcing untreated sewage into drinking water supplies.

Climate Facts

- In Africa, about 40 billion hours of labor are wasted each year in collecting drinking water from far-off places.

- In developing countries, the average daily water usage of a person is 2.64 gallons (9.4 l), whereas in the United States it varies from 100 to 175 gallons (378 to 662 l).

Polar Regions

The Arctic Circle in the northern hemisphere and the Antarctic Circle in the southern hemisphere are the polar regions. While the Arctic is a frozen ocean surrounded by land, Antarctica is an ice-covered continent. The Arctic is warming twice as fast as other parts of the world. The average temperature in Alaska has increased by 5.4°F (3.0°C) since 1970.

The Arctic Ice Melt

Ice has a greater tendency to reflect sunrays (called albedo) than ocean or land. Thus, the Arctic ice melt is causing more sunlight absorption by the earth. This is contributing to global warming. Melting glaciers are also adding to the rise in seal levels and affecting people living on the coasts. **Biodiversity** is also suffering since migratory birds are heavily dependent on the Arctic regions for feeding and breeding. Polar bears and many seal species are on the verge of extinction.

Antarctica

Climate change is having a disastrous effect on Antarctica. The sea ice is decreasing rapidly, with a 2018 study showing the rate had tripled since 2013. Krill populations that feed on algae found underneath sea ice are decreasing, too, which in turn is affecting the population of Adélie penguins that feed on krill. In the last 50 years, the temperature of the region has increased by about 5.4°F (3°C). About 240 billion tons are now lost each year.

Climate Facts

- In 2000, the Ward Hunt Ice Shelf, which for 3,000 years was the single largest ice block in the Arctic, cracked. Within two years, it split in half due to rising temperatures.

- Since 1950, the Antarctic Peninsula's temperature has risen by 4.5 °F (2.5°C).

What Is Climate Change? 37

International Treaties

Several countries have come together to find ways to control climate change. They have formed treaties, agreeing to reduce pollution and the emission of GHGs. Developed and industrialized countries, such as the United States, are among the most GHG-producing countries. Hence, they have a greater responsibility toward the environment.

UNFCCC

In June 1992, the United Nations Framework Convention on Climate Change (UNFCCC) was signed by about 150 countries at Rio de Janeiro, Brazil. It went into effect in March 1994. The main purpose of this agreement is to control the GHG content in the air. This would reduce the impact of man-made activities on the global climate system. However, this treaty does not put any limits on harmful emissions by any nation.

Kyoto Protocol

In December 1997, an agreement related to climate change called the Kyoto **Protocol** was signed in Kyoto, Japan. It was enforced 8 years later in February 2005. According to this protocol, by 2012, 37 industrialized countries were required to cut down their emissions of methane, sulfur hexafluoride, carbon dioxide, hydrofluorocarbons, and nitrous oxide by 5.2 percent.

Paris Agreement

In 2015, more than 190 countries met and agreed on the Paris Agreement, an international treaty designed to prevent global temperatures from rising more than 2°C before the end of the century. It was the largest and most expansive treaty to save the world ever written. In 2017, however, its future was put in doubt when President Donald Trump pulled the United States out of the agreement. The U.S. is the largest producer of greenhouse gases. Though almost all other nations continue to work to live up to its goals, the future of the Agreement is in doubt.

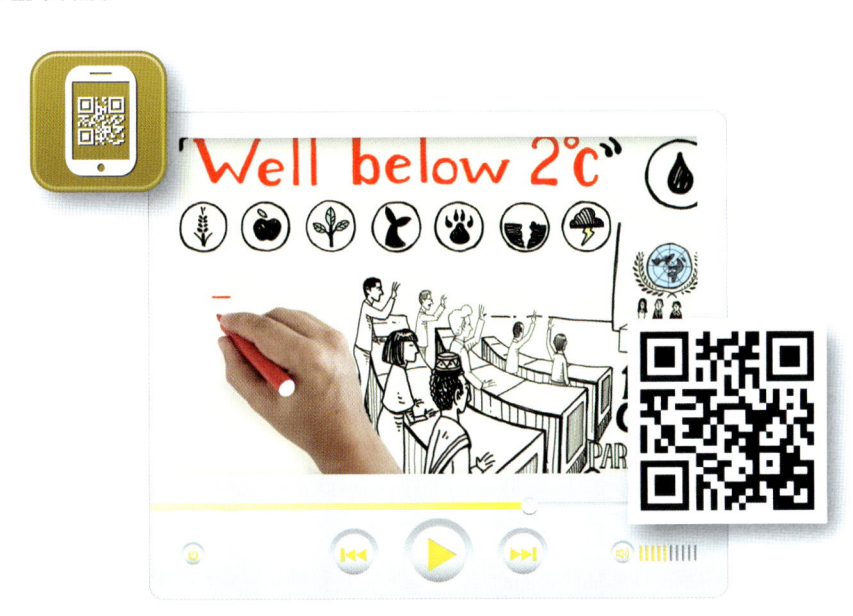

The Paris Agreement explained

Climate Facts

- Presently, the UNFCCC has 194 member countries.

- 191 countries have signed the Kyoto Protocol.

What Is Climate Change?

Climate in the Future

Predicting future climate change is not easy. There are fewer chances that harmful emissions will be brought under control to stabilize global temperatures. Keeping in view the current situation, the Intergovernmental Panel on Climate Change (IPCC), an organization that assesses global information on climate change, has made certain predictions about climatic effects.

Rise in GHGs

The emission of GHGs in the atmosphere is on the rise. The IPCC predicts that by 2100 CO_2 concentration in the atmosphere will increase by 41 to 158 percent, depending on the location. The concentration of the remaining GHGs will increase from 9 billion metric in 1990 to 13 billion metric tons by 2020.

Rising Sea Levels

The IPCC predicts that by 2100, the average global sea level may increase by 7.2 to 23.6 in. This estimate excludes the ice sheet flow. This prediction is made keeping in mind the 6.6-inch (0.17-m) global average sea rise in the twentieth century.

Rising Temperature

According to the IPCC, by 2100, the global average surface temperature will rise by 2° to 11.5°F (1.1 to 6.38°C) in comparison to 3.2° to 7.2°F (1.77 to 4°C) during 1980-90. The regions near the Arctic Circle will be warmer because melted ice in the Arctic will absorb more sunlight.

Climate Facts

- From 1906–2005, the global average surface temperature rose by 1.3°F (0.74°C).

- Since 1978, Arctic sea ice has reduced 2.7 percent every 10 years.

What Is Climate Change?

Adaptation

Climate change is a continuous phenomenon. Even if efforts were made to control and stabilize GHGs, the global temperatures would still rise by 1.8°F (1°C) by the end of the 21st century. This change cannot be reversed since the atmosphere already has high levels of GHGs. Therefore, adapting to the changing climate is an ecological necessity.

Features of Adaptive Measures

Adaptation measures are not foolproof and they cost a lot, as in the case of **dikes** and **bulkheads** built on shores to protect coastal property from rising sea levels, for example. These measures should be flexible enough to accommodate any new development due to climate change. Some adaptive strategies already being enforced worldwide include the construction of climate-proof buildings, and investment in drought-resistant systems that safeguard water and food during times of disaster.

CLIMATE CHANGE: Problems and Progress

Adaptation in Developing Countries

Developed nations, which are the chief source of GHG emissions, have greater adaptation capabilities. In contrast, developing nations that do not contribute much to the changing climate do not have adequate monetary funds to implement adaptation strategies. These nations with already inadequate food and water resources are becoming more prone to disastrous heat waves, floods, and hurricanes. Many funds have been established to help the Least Developed Countries (LDCs) to enforce urgent adaptation requirements.

Adaptation Measures

Individuals, communities, and organizations can help to control climate change by following some adaptation measures, which are as follows:

- Produce crops that are more tolerant to heat, drought, and waterlogging from heavy rainfall or flooding.
- Provide more shade to livestock during summers by improving the airflow in barns.
- Improve evacuation routes for low-lying areas to save people during times of flooding and sea storms.
- Protect and improve migration corridors for animals to allow them a safe migration.
- Plant more trees and build green spaces in urban settings to offset the heat.

Climate Facts

- The Adaptation Fund, started in 2007 under the Kyoto Protocol, is a fund to help developing countries cope with climate change.

- Australia gave $150 million from 2008-11 under its International Climate Change Adaptation Initiative (ICCAI) program to help needy countries.

TEXT-DEPENDENT QUESTIONS

1. What is the greenhouse effect?

2. Describe some effects of El Niño or La Niña.

3. What natural disasters are increasing because of climate change?

4. What is coral bleaching and what causes it?

5. Why is ocean acidification a bad thing for the planet?

6. What is being lost at the polar regions due to climate change?

7. What was the goal of the Kyoto Protocol?

8. Where is the ozone hole?

RESEARCH PROJECTS

1. Read articles from your local media about climate change effects in your area. What are the main issues your area needs to watch? What steps are local governments taking to ease the problem?

2. Read about "climate change deniers." What are the reasons that they use to choose to ignore the science and the state of climate change. Write a poster or Power Point to show them the facts.

3. Read about the Paris Agreement and about the United States decision to back out of it. What were the reasons President Trump gave? Do you agree with them? If not, why not? Write a letter to the president expressing your views.

FIND OUT MORE

Books

Collins, Anna. *The Climate Change Crisis.* Minneapolis: Lucent Books, 2018.

Gitlin, Marty (ed.) *Our Climate Future (Issues That Concern You).* Farmington Hills, MI: Greenhaven Press, 2018.

Swanson, Jennifer. *Geoengineering Earth's Climate: Resetting the Thermostat.* New York: Twenty-First Century Books, 2018.

On the Internet

Defenders of Wildlife
defenders.org/climate-change/overview

Climate Change overview
worldbank.org/en/topic/climatechange/overview

National Geographic Climate Change Overview
nationalgeographic.com/environment/global-warming/global-warming-overview/

SERIES GLOSSARY OF KEY TERMS

bioaccumulation the process of the buildup of toxic chemical substances in the body

biodiversity the diversity of plant and animal life in a habitat (or in the world as a whole)

ecosystem refers to a community of organisms, their interaction with each other, and their physical environment

famine a severe shortage of food (as through crop failure), resulting in hunger, starvation, and death

hydrophobic tending to repel, and not absorb water or become wet by water

irrigation the method of providing water to agricultural fields

La Niña periodic, significant cooling of the surface waters of the equatorial Pacific Ocean, which causes abnormal weather patterns

migration the movement of persons or animals from one country or locality to another

pollutants the foreign materials which are harmful to the environment

precipitation the falling to earth of any form of water (rain, snow, hail, sleet, or mist)

stressors processes or events that cause stress

susceptible yielding readily to or capable of

symbiotic the interaction between organisms (especially of different species) that live together and happen to benefit from each other

vulnerable someone or something that can be easily harmed or attacked

INDEX

adaptation, 42-43
agriculture, 9, 24-25, 34
amphibians, 27
Antarctica, 37
Arctic hole, 12
Arctic ice melt, 36
birds, 27, 36
carbon dioxide, 10-11, 18-19, 25, 40
climate change
causes of, 14-17
future of, 40-43
history of, 8-9
threats, 20-21
coral reefs, 28-29
crops, 24-25, 43
deforestation, 18
diseases, 20-21
drinking water, 34-35
droughts, 23
Earth's orbit, 14

El Niño, 16-17
fish, 27
floods, 23
forests, 30-31
fossil fuels, 18
glaciers, 32, 34, 36
global warming, 17, 26, 36
Great Barrier Reef, 29
greenhouse gases (GHGs), 10, 18-19, 40, 42-43
heat waves, 22
hibernation, 26
human activities, 10, 18-19
hurricanes, 23
ice age, 9
ice sheets, 32
Kyoto Protocol, 38
La Niña, 16-17
mammals, 26

man-made GHGs, 10, 12
Montreal Protocol, 12
natural disasters, 22-23
nitrous oxide, 10
oceans, 32-33, 35-37, 41
organizations, 40
overpopulation, 18
ozone hole, 12-13
Paris agreement, 39
polar regions, 36-37
precipitation, 23, 25
sea levels, 33, 35, 41
solar variations, 15
Tibet ozone hole, 13
treaties, 38-39
UNFCC, 38
UV rays, 12
weather events, 17
wildlife, 26-27

Photo Credits

Photographs sourced by Macaw Media, except for: Dreamstime.com: John Wollwerth, 25. Shutterstock/Photomontage, 41.